From Fail to Win!
Learning from Bad Ideas

MEDICINE

Rebecca Vickers

Raintree

Chicago, Illinois

www.heinemannraintree.com
Visit our website to find out more information about Heinemann-Raintree books.

To order:
☎ Phone 888-454-2279
🖥 Visit www.heinemannraintree.com to browse our catalog and order online.

Edited by Andrew Farrow, Vaarunika Dharmapala, and Adrian Vigliano
Designed by Richard Parker
Picture research by Mica Brancic

Originated by Capstone Global Library Ltd
Printed and bound in China by South China Printing Company Ltd

14 13 12 11 10
10 9 8 7 6 5 4 3 2 1

Library of Congress Cataloging-in-Publication Data
Vickers, Rebecca.
  Medicine / Rebecca Vickers.
     p. cm.—(From Fail to Win)
  Includes bibliographical references and index.
  ISBN 978-1-4109-3908-1 (hc)
  1. Medical misconceptions—Popular works. I. Title.
  R729.9.V53 2011
  610—dc22
                                   2010001464

Acknowledgments
The author and publisher are grateful to the following for permission to reproduce copyright material: Alamy pp. **13** (© Feije Riemersma), **34** (© Interfoto), **41** (© The Print Collector); Corbis pp. **5** (© Peter M. Fisher), **8** (BSIP/© B. Boissonnet), **9** (© Bettmann), **17** (© Bettmann), **19** (cultura/© Ghislain & Marie David de Lossy), **21** (© Bettmann), **26** (dpa/© dpa), **28** (© Bettmann), **31** (© Image Source), **27** (© Richard T. Nowitz), **37** (© EdKashi2004); Getty Images pp. **6** (The Bridgeman Art Library/M. Albik), **15** (Hulton Archive/Fox Photos/Harry Shepherd), **20** (Time Life Pictures/Stan Wayman), **23** (AFP/Dieter Nagl), **25** (The Bridgeman Art Library/Gaston Melingue), **33** (Time Life Pictures/Mansell), **36** (General Photographic Agency), **39** (De Agostini Picture Library), **43** (AFP Photo/Torsten Blackwood), **44** (The Bridgeman Art Library/Theodor Rombouts), **47** (Hulton Archive), **49** (Hulton Archive/Gemma Levine); Science & Society Picture Library p. **29** (Daily Herald Archive at the National Media Museum); Science Photo Library p. **40** (Sheila Terry); Wellcome Library, London pp. **10** (Wellcome Images), **42** (Wellcome Images).

Cover photograph of a bedridden patient accompanied by a nurse, on the roof of Albert Dock Hospital, overlooking Docklands, in London, September 22, 1938, reproduced with permission of Getty Images (Fox Photos).

We would like to thank Ann Fullick for her invaluable help in the preparation of this book.

Every effort has been made to contact copyright holders of material reproduced in this book. Any omissions will be rectified in subsequent printings if notice is given to the publisher.

Disclaimer
All the Internet addresses (URLs) given in this book were valid at the time of going to press. However, due to the dynamic nature of the Internet, some addresses may have changed, or sites may have changed or ceased to exist since publication. While the author and publisher regret any inconvenience this may cause readers, no responsibility for any such changes can be accepted by either the author or the publisher.

Contents

Any words appearing in the text in bold, **like this**, are explained in the glossary.

Lessons Learned

In the past, when doctors became qualified to practice medicine, they swore an **oath** known as the Hippocratic Oath. Today, many doctors swear a modern version of this. They make promises about how they will perform their duties. Hippocrates, the ancient Greek doctor for whom the oath was named, said, "First, do no harm." This seems obvious—doctors and the methods they use are supposed to make people feel better or cure them.

However, things do not always go as planned. In medicine, as in other fields, knowledge improves over time. New discoveries are made and old ideas have to be discarded. Sometimes, though, incorrect theories become accepted and are put into action, or other mistakes are made. In medicine this can lead to people being **misdiagnosed**, suffering unnecessarily, and even dying.

This book covers 10 areas where the medical profession got it wrong, what happened, and the lessons that were learned. In some cases, learning from these failures has pushed forward the frontiers of medicine and led to successes, improved understanding, and treatments that have saved lives.

Why do things go wrong?

Three of the main reasons why doctors get things wrong are:

- Lack of knowledge: In the past, mistakes were made or the wrong path was followed because medical and scientific knowledge had not developed enough to understand a condition or treatment.

- Flawed research: When a new medical theory, procedure, or treatment is being developed, research takes place to make sure the idea is correct or the treatment is safe. When this research is not done properly, there can be dangerous consequences.

- Human error: Sometimes people make mistakes. When doctors make mistakes, the results can be deadly.

From fail to win

All medical mistakes and failures can be dangerous, but some have been more disastrous than others. The medical failures in this book are counted down from 10 to 1. Number one is the most damaging or worst idea from which we have learned the most. This is our list—do you agree with the choices?

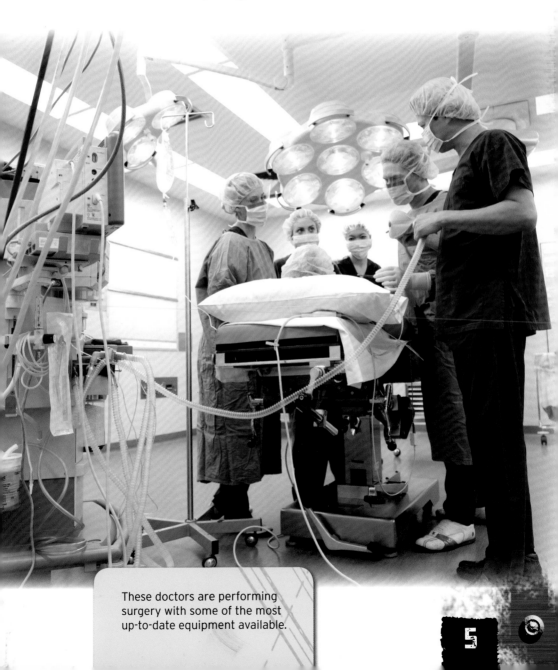

These doctors are performing surgery with some of the most up-to-date equipment available.

Urine: From Guesswork to Lab Work

When you describe your symptoms to your doctor, it is up to him or her to figure out what is wrong with you. For hundreds of years, one of the main **diagnostic** methods was the examination of urine. Everyone produced urine, it required no special procedure to collect it, and it could be looked at, smelled, and even tasted!

Color, smell, and taste

Looking at urine to diagnose medical conditions is known as uroscopy. Over 3,000 years ago in ancient India and Egypt, doctors and holy people used urine to diagnose and predict. By the **Middle Ages**, doctors had discovered very detailed uroscopic diagnosis methods, with special glass collection jars and charts. It was believed that the color of the urine could help doctors to decide what illnesses their patients suffered from. The taste and smell of the urine were also used to identify various diseases.

This chart from the 15th century shows several jars of differently colored urine.

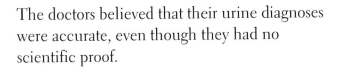

The doctors believed that their urine diagnoses were accurate, even though they had no scientific proof.

Doctors in the Middle Ages also thought that the various layers of urine in a collection jar related to specific areas of the body. The top layer related to the head, the next layer down related to the upper torso, the next layer to the abdomen, and the bottom layer to the urinary system and sex organs.

Depending on urine

Despite its widespread use, people began to question the use of urine diagnosis as early as the 16th and 17th centuries.

Despite this, uroscopy continued to be used as a diagnostic tool—for example, in the diagnosis of diabetes. In fact, the scientific name for diabetes, *Diabetes mellitus*, translates from Latin as "honey-sweet urine"!

Uromancy: More magic than medicine

Some people tried to make money out of urine diagnosis. During the Middle Ages, these people, known as uromancers, practiced the art of uromancy. They claimed that not only could they diagnose diseases by examining urine, but that they could also predict the future, like someone reading tea leaves!

George III's blue urine

King George III of England (1738–1820) is known to have suffered from bouts of "madness." It is recorded that sometimes, during his periods of insanity, he produced blue urine, to the amazement of his doctors.

Today, some medical researchers think he suffered from the disease porphyria, which can sometimes cause blue urine. Others think that the blue color was just the result of medicine made from the blue-colored flower, gentian, which he took for indigestion.

What was learned?

As early as the 16th century, some doctors were starting to doubt the effectiveness of urine diagnosis by color, taste, and smell. However, it was not until the start of laboratory-based testing methods in the 19th and 20th centuries that the accurate use of urine as a diagnostic tool came into its own.

Although the healers of ancient times were right that urine could tell them a lot about a person's condition and health, their methods and beliefs usually gave them the wrong answers. For example, in ancient Egypt it was believed that you could tell whether a woman was pregnant by pouring her urine onto plant seeds and checking their growth. Despite their mistakes, they were right that urine could be used. Today, most women confirm their pregnancies at a very early stage using a urine-testing method. Urine is also used to test for diabetes, kidney function, blood pressure problems, and the use of legal and illegal drugs.

This technician is preparing urine samples for analysis. Urine analysis is one of the ways that athletes are tested for the use of illegal or performance-enhancing drugs.

WIN!

The Chamberlen Forceps: A Case of Professional Jealousy

In the late 16th century, a French family named Chamberlen immigrated to England to escape religious persecution. For five generations various members of the family worked as surgeons, doctors, and midwives. Over the years, their reputation for saving women who were having difficulties in childbirth grew. This was not just good luck. The Chamberlen family had a secret.

Improved, not invented

For some time doctors, midwives, and others who helped women give birth had known that a woman and her child could be saved if a baby stuck in the birth canal during a delivery could be gently pulled out. Various instruments were used to help in this process. They included metal forceps with wide, solid, curved blades joined by two handles. This instrument was sometimes effective, but often the woman or baby was fatally injured by the forceps. Because of this, it was only used in very dangerous circumstances in which the mother or baby was unlikely to survive.

The Chamberlen family had a secret weapon in the battle to get mother and child through a birth safely and uninjured. They had made a greatly improved version of the forceps.

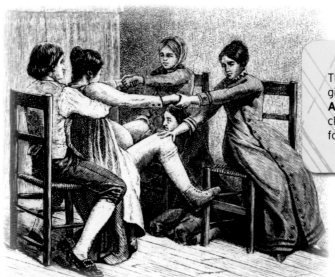

This drawing shows a woman giving birth in **colonial America**. Until the last century, childbirth was very dangerous for both mother and baby.

Professional jealousy

The Chamberlen forceps were in two parts, so that each side could be gently inserted and placed around the baby's head. The flat, curved blades were not solid metal, but were loops with a hole in the middle. Mothers and their children helped by the Chamberlen forceps were much more likely to survive.

The sad fact is that this amazing breakthrough in forceps design only benefited a few women over a 100-year period. The members of the Chamberlen family kept their forceps a secret and only used them on those who could afford to pay their high fees. Their **professional jealousy** and desire for wealth was stronger than their desire to help all women during the dangerous hours of childbirth. It was not until after the death of Dr. Hugh Chamberlen in 1728 that the design became public and its use spread. The design of the **obstetric** forceps used by doctors today is almost identical to that of the last of the Chamberlens' secret instruments.

This drawing shows two versions of the Chamberlen forceps.

WIN!

Failure to give access to success

The Chamberlens' development of forceps was a great success, with an innovative design that has stood the test of time. It was also a huge failure. By keeping such an important breakthrough to themselves and a small number of patients in one country, the Chamberlen family slowed medical progress and probably allowed many thousands of women and children to die. Money and the desire for fame won out over human life.

What has been learned?

Today, information about new medical techniques and procedures is published and made available to the medical profession worldwide. This is considered to be part of the **ethics** of the profession. While the ideas are freely available, the use of new discoveries is limited by their cost and how easy they are to get hold of. In some countries, government controls or health insurance provisions may keep patients from having specific treatments.

In the developing world, poverty often limits access to life-saving drugs and equipment. One example of this is the case of the drugs used for the treatment of **HIV/AIDS**. For a number of years, sufferers in the developed world have had access to the retroviral drugs used to treat this condition. This has not been the case in the developing world. Lack of money, of correct storage conditions, and of medical support, as well as political corruption and a lack of education, means treatment is hardest to get in those areas where it is needed most.

Controlling discoveries in the 21st century

While the medical profession tries to share its new discoveries, there are now others accused of protecting their finds. For example, many **pharmaceutical** companies and other researchers attempt to **patent** biological compounds or even individual **genes**. They say they are protecting their investments and that unless there is financial reward, companies will not even look for new drugs or cures. Others say they care more about money than helping people. Whom do you agree with?

Fresh-Air Treatments

Imagine having a terrible condition in which every breath you take turns into a hacking cough. Eventually you become weaker and start coughing up blood. All the doctors can suggest is that you get plenty of fresh air. If you are rich enough, you can go to stay in a **sanatorium**, a cross between a hotel and a hospital, but for most people this is out of the question.

You gradually lose weight, get more and more tired, and never stop coughing. As you grow weaker, the disease becomes stronger and harder to shake off. It might take a few years, but death is usually the final outcome.

Killer TB

U.S. TB death rates:

late
1800s: 1 in 7 of
     all deaths

1920: About
     120,000 deaths

2006: 644 deaths

The scourge of consumption

This was the situation for people suffering from what was called "consumption," but is now known as tuberculosis (TB). When TB first became a major killer of **epidemic** proportions in the late 18th century, doctors had various theories about what caused it.

It was the time of the **Industrial Revolution** and the growth of crowded city environments. Many doctors connected the increase in deaths from consumption to the overcrowding, polluted air, and bad nutrition of urban workers and their families.

Overcrowded living and working conditions did contribute to the likelihood of developing a severe, fatal case of TB. However, being middle class or rich was not a protection from this disease. By the 1830s the medical belief in the effectiveness of fresh-air treatments for tuberculosis was growing, partly because there were no other options.

Good dying young

During the 19th century the world lost a number of young, talented writers, artists, and musicians to the scourge of TB. These are believed to have included the poets John Keats and Edgar Allan Poe, novelist Emily Brontë, and composers Frédéric Chopin and Stephen Foster. John Keats followed the recommendation of his doctor to go to Italy for the warm air, but he died there of TB, at only 25 years of age.

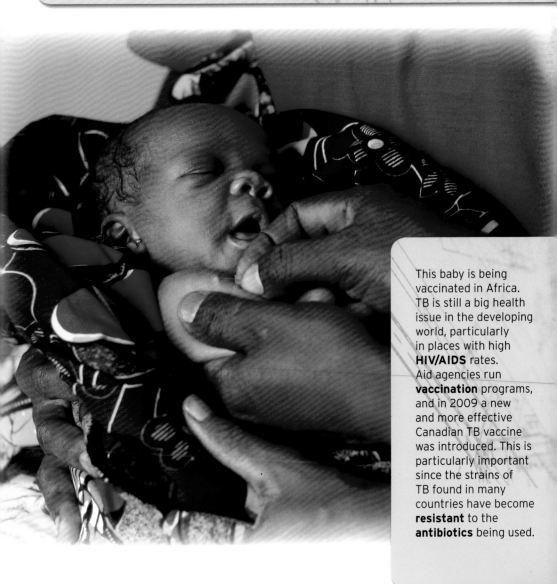

This baby is being vaccinated in Africa. TB is still a big health issue in the developing world, particularly in places with high **HIV/AIDS** rates. Aid agencies run **vaccination** programs, and in 2009 a new and more effective Canadian TB vaccine was introduced. This is particularly important since the strains of TB found in many countries have become **resistant** to the **antibiotics** being used.

Warm air, cool air, or pine-scented air?

During the first half of the 19th century, doctors in Great Britain recommended that their wealthy patients head for southern Europe, where they said the warm air could slow down or even cure consumption. Unfortunately, the cemeteries of Italy are full of hopeful British TB sufferers who died far from home. By the 1850s, with deaths from TB still rising, medical ideas shifted and doctors came to believe that cool, fresh air was better for those with TB. British patients who could afford it went off to Germany or Switzerland.

The open-air cure

The number of sanatoriums offering open-air cures expanded in the early 20th century. Governments and charities started to pay for poor people to go for fresh-air treatments at special sanatoriums. Most people who contracted TB still died or were sick for a very long time.

In the United States, Dr. John Croghan, who owned the Mammoth Cave complex in Kentucky, moved many TB sufferers into the "cool and pure air" of the caves. He swore by this treatment, but most of his patients died. Some German doctors, such as Hermann Brehmer, believed that the scent from pine forests could also improve TB symptoms. However, more patients kept coming, and many died.

What was learned?

In 1882 the German medical researcher Robert Koch conclusively proved that tuberculosis was an infectious disease caused by the **bacteria** *Mycobacterium tuberculosis*. The fresh air—warm or cool—and rest that patients received in sanatoriums probably made them stronger and more able to fight disease, but it would never be able to cure a bacterial infection. Sanatoriums also had the added benefit of isolating active TB cases from the rest of the population.

There was still no cure, so doctors continued to push the fresh-air option. In sanatoriums for children, there were open-air schools, and some even had open-air chapels.

These TB patients are being treated outdoors in the snow in 1933.

Pills and shots win out

During the second half of the 20th century, the outlook for TB sufferers changed completely. Antibiotics had been developed to treat and cure many bacterial infections, including TB. A vaccination developed in 1921 became widely available after World War II (1939–1945). Hundreds of sanatoriums closed, and the idea of fresh-air therapy became a concept of the past.

Lobotomies: Deactivating the Brain

Medical professionals today admit that surprisingly little is really understood about how the brain works. Around 80 years ago the medical profession knew even less. This did not, however, stop doctors from developing and using a technique that involved cutting out a section of the brain.

In the 1930s a Portuguese surgeon, António Egas Moniz, perfected a method of disrupting nerve fibers in the front of the brain, the prefrontal cortex. This procedure became known as a lobotomy. At the time, the doctors were concerned that there were very few options for treating people suffering from mental illness. Large mental hospitals, called asylums, virtually imprisoned the mentally ill, with little chance of their conditions improving. Some doctors and psychiatrists thought the only hope for these patients was some form of surgery.

Freeman and Watts

Two U.S. doctors, psychiatrist Walter Freeman and surgeon James Watts, wanted to create a surgical technique that was simple enough to be performed in mental asylums. They hoped that such an operation might improve patients' conditions to the point where they would be able to leave the hospital. During the 1940s they improved on previous lobotomy techniques. Eventually Freeman came up with the idea of performing a type of lobotomy that did not require a full operation, but could be done through the top of the eye sockets using ice picks and a small rubber hammer. Parts of the frontal lobe were damaged, but not cut away. Freeman recommended this form of lobotomy for a very wide range of conditions, from **schizophrenia**, serious depression, and violence to anxiety, moodiness, and misbehavior in children.

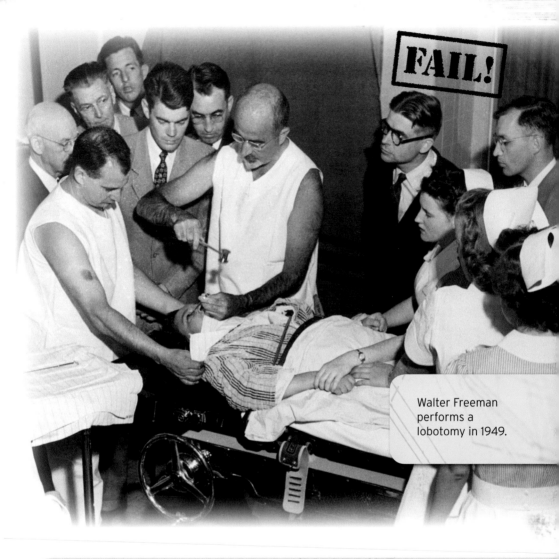

FAIL!

Walter Freeman performs a lobotomy in 1949.

A sexist treatment

In some places as many as 85 percent of the mental patients treated with a lobotomy were women. Why was this the case? There are many possible reasons. Culturally and socially, women were expected to meet different standards of behavior than men. For example, a man who had violent tendencies, had a lot of interest in sex, and swore a lot would not be seen as mentally ill, but in the 1930s a woman with these characteristics might have been.

Why perform lobotomies?

Lobotomies rapidly became an accepted way of dealing with conditions for which there previously had been no treatment besides close confinement, straitjackets, and isolation. After a lobotomy procedure, a patient who had been aggressive and hard to manage was usually much calmer, but the side effects could be horrific and were irreversible. These included intellectual impairment, personality change, epilepsy, **incontinence**, and even complete loss of social skills. Critics referred to these patients as being like zombies. By the 1950s lobotomies were being widely performed, particularly in the United States, the United Kingdom, and Scandinavia. It is estimated that about 40,000 lobotomies were performed in the United States, 17,000 in the United Kingdom, and about 9,300 in Scandinavian countries.

What was learned?

From the very beginning of its use, the lobotomy had critics. However, it still became acceptable and widespread. It was only when other treatment options became available that almost overnight the lobotomy started to be seen as a failed remedy. The development of effective **antipsychotic** drugs during the 1960s was the first blow. This type of treatment was also a physical attempt to influence the brain, but it was less invasive and seemed to have fewer side effects.

With many mental hospitals still full of aging lobotomized patients with blank faces and poor brain function, the critics had a lot of ammunition. Lobotomies were now seen as scandalous and called "torture."

A Nobel Prize for Moniz

In 1949 the Portuguese pioneer of lobotomy surgery, Dr. António Egas Moniz, received the Nobel Prize for Medicine in recognition of his work. This was seen as confirming the prefrontal lobotomy as a reasonable and acceptable medical procedure. In the three years that followed this award, more lobotomies were carried out around the world than the total previously performed.

By the 1970s and 1980s, the number of lobotomies performed dropped from thousands to hundreds worldwide. Today, there are even fewer. The lobotomy has now been rejected as a technique and discredited by the medical profession.

Talking is good

Today, the most popular treatments for mental illnesses are those that focus on the life experiences, personal relationships, and environment of the patient. Being able to control one's own thoughts and behavior is seen as a way to achieve real improvement. This has led to the growth in importance of **cognitive behavioral therapy (CBT)**. This technique can be used individually with a therapist or as part of a group.

The group sessions used in cognitive behavioral therapy give people the chance to share their problems and worries with each other.

Thalidomide: Pharmaceutical Failure

Morning sickness, or the nausea and vomiting that many women suffer in the early months of pregnancy, is unpleasant, but gradually eases off. For some, however, it is much worse, with the nausea and vomiting lasting all day and for many months. This can lead to **anemia** and other conditions that are a threat to the mother and her unborn child. In the 1950s doctors were delighted when they discovered that a new drug made by a German **pharmaceutical** company seemed to stop all the symptoms of morning sickness. The name of the drug was thalidomide.

Development of a "wonder drug"

Researchers claimed that thalidomide could be used for a number of conditions, including depression, headaches, and nausea. It was recognized as a painkiller and a sedative. From 1957 it was prescribed for the treatment of morning sickness.

This child's mother was prescribed thalidomide during her pregnancy. As a result, the child was born with small, stunted arms.

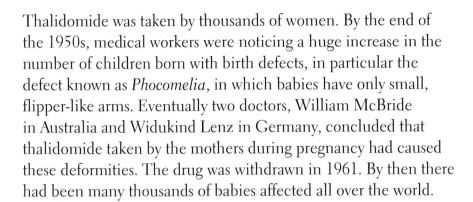

Thalidomide was taken by thousands of women. By the end of the 1950s, medical workers were noticing a huge increase in the number of children born with birth defects, in particular the defect known as *Phocomelia*, in which babies have only small, flipper-like arms. Eventually two doctors, William McBride in Australia and Widukind Lenz in Germany, concluded that thalidomide taken by the mothers during pregnancy had caused these deformities. The drug was withdrawn in 1961. By then there had been many thousands of babies affected all over the world.

Dr. Frances Kelsey: FDA heroine

Between 1957 and 1961, thousands of babies around the world were born with rare deformities. Some did not survive. In the United States, however, only 17 children were born with thalidomide damage. This small number is due to the actions of one woman, an employee of the U.S. Food and Drug Administration (FDA), Dr. Frances Kelsey. She was not convinced that enough testing had been done on thalidomide and refused to license it for use within the United States.

Dr. Kelsey was later hailed as a heroine for standing firm against approval. In 1962 she was awarded the President's Award for Distinguished Federal Civilian Service by John F. Kennedy. Kelsey continued her work for the FDA, retiring at age 90 in 2005.

What went wrong?

Why did the medical profession and the pharmaceutical industry fail to realize what would happen? There are three main reasons:

- It was widely believed that drugs did not pass from a mother into the baby because of the barrier of the **placenta**. This was wrong, and now most women are recommended to use as few medical products as possible during pregnancy and, if necessary, to do so only under the instructions of a doctor. It is now understood that the developing fetus is particularly sensitive to harm during the first three months of a pregnancy.
- The testing of drugs before they were released on to the market was much less stringent then than it is now. In fact, the thalidomide tragedy was directly responsible for the tightening up of drug approval systems throughout the world.
- It was not understood how important it was for doctors to report any unusual outbreaks of diseases or clusters of birth defects. Today, medical authorities would realize much more quickly if there were a similar occurrence of rare deformities on such a large scale.

What has been learned?

Despite its tragic past, there is now a growing recognition that thalidomide can in certain circumstances be an effective treatment. It can be used as pain relief in the disease leprosy and to treat multiple myeloma, a kind of blood cancer. Research is being carried out to test its effectiveness in treating over 30 other diseases and conditions.

Even so, doctors and governments are taking no chances. The use of thalidomide is highly controlled. In the United States, a special process, the System for Thalidomide Education and Prescribing Safety (STEPS), is used in every case to decide if it is safe to use the drug. In some developing countries the controls are not tight enough. Pregnant women who take the drug are still at risk of giving birth to babies with defects.

Bass-baritone singer Thomas Quasthoff (right) is applauded by fellow singer Placido Domingo (left). Quasthoff was born with thalidomide-related birth defects. He has gone on to become one of the most accomplished singers in the world.

Vaccines: Experimenting on Patients

Inoculation

By the 18th century, infectious smallpox had become the leading killer disease in the world. Most people who caught it died, and those who survived were usually left with pitted scars from the rash. Many became blind. During the 18th century, **inoculation**, catching a mild form of the disease on purpose, had become popular. This was because it was observed that once people survived smallpox, they usually did not get it again. We now know that this is because our **immune system** creates chemicals called antibodies that prevent us from catching some diseases more than once. The big risk with inoculation was that the patient might develop a bad case and die.

When doctors, medical researchers, or **pharmaceutical** companies have an idea for a treatment or cure today, there are rules that have to be followed before the treatment can be tried out on patients. These strictly enforced regulations have increased over the years, particularly after well-publicized tragedies, such as the disastrous use of thalidomide by pregnant women (see pages 20–23). It is now seen as part of the code of medical **ethics** that people are protected from a new medicine or type of treatment until it has been tested as much as is possible. This was certainly not the case in the late 18th century, when **vaccinations** were first developed.

Observation, hypothesis, experimentation

Edward Jenner was a country doctor in England. In his local area, there was a disease called cowpox, a mild form of smallpox. People believed that when milkmaids had suffered from cowpox, they never caught smallpox. Having observed that this was true, Jenner decided the only way to test his **hypothesis** was through an experiment. He had no ethics committee to run his idea by, or any government agency likely to come knocking at his door. So Jenner just chose a small boy and started his experiment.

"Guinea pig" James Phipps

Probably no one would have ever heard of James Phipps if he had not been the healthy eight-year-old boy Dr. Jenner chose for his smallpox experiment in 1796. After collecting pus from a cowpox scab on the skin of a milkmaid suffering from the mild disease, Jenner cut Phipps's arm and inserted the pus. Phipps contracted the disease and was a bit sick for two or three days, but made a full recovery. Then the experiment took what could have been a very dangerous turn. Jenner infected the young boy with pus from a scab on the skin of a real smallpox sufferer. If the cowpox infection did not act as a protection from the deadly disease, it was likely that James Phipps would catch smallpox and die. As Jenner reported, "No disease followed." His hypothesis had been proven correct.

In this painting, Edward Jenner is shown performing the world's first vaccination.

What was learned?

Edward Jenner and James Phipps were lucky that his experiment had succeeded and opened the door for the development and use of smallpox vaccinations. Over the next 184 years the technique was improved, and its use spread around the world. Smallpox was declared officially eradicated in 1980. Millions have been saved from a painful and deadly disease.

Doctors and other scientific researchers have often worked around the dilemma of how to experiment to prove their theories. They have used themselves, their families, and their employees as "guinea pigs." During the last century, prisoners, soldiers, and, infamously, inmates of Nazi concentration camps have become part of medical research. Some of these people agreed to take part, but others either had no say or were given limited or even false information about the risks involved.

The Nuremberg Trials were held after World War II to bring Nazi officers, doctors, and others to justice. This witness at the trials was imprisoned in a concentration camp and experimented on without her consent.

Testing on animals: Cruel or necessary?

While it is now prohibited to use people with no control over their lives as part of medical experimentation in most places, a new dilemma has arisen. For hundreds of years, medical and scientific researchers used animals as part of their studies and experiments. However, during the last 50 years there has been a growing campaign to stop experimenting on animals, including the procedure known as **vivisection**. Those who oppose animal testing, particularly tests done to gain marketing approval for luxury products such as cosmetics and perfumes, consider it cruel and unnecessary. They do not think that the knowledge gained by the tests or experiments justifies the suffering caused to the animals. So, questions of ethics still surround research.

Paid to take a risk

In 2006 the shocking news broke that six men taking part in a drug trial had been hospitalized. The trial, for a new drug called TGN1412, had only just started when the volunteers became critically ill. The drug had caused their immune systems to attack their internal organs. At first it was thought that at least two would not survive, but all were out of the hospital after a month. Doctors believe they may never fully recover, with possible permanent damage to their immune systems. Fortunately this kind of extreme reaction is rare.

Rats are often used in medical research because they have similar **genes** to humans. This means that scientists can tell a lot about how a human will react to a disease from the way a rat does.

Radium and Radioactive Treatments

When in 1895 the German scientist Wilhelm Roentgen made an X-ray image of his wife's hand, the age of medical uses for radiation had begun. In 1898, in France, Marie and Pierre Curie discovered the radioactive elements radium and polonium. Marie Curie went on to work on the chemistry of radioactive elements and their medical application. Both Roentgen and the Curies received the Nobel Prize for their discoveries. However, their brilliant discoveries led to some very bad ideas.

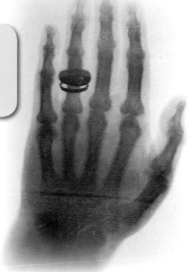

This is the first X-ray photograph ever made. It shows the hand of Wilhelm Roentgen's wife.

Crazy for radium

Within 20 years of the discovery of radioactive elements, medical professionals and the public seemed obsessed with the possible curative properties of radium. Particularly in the United States, radium cures were recommended for everything from constipation and high blood pressure to arthritis and cancer. During the 1920s two radium products became popular. The first was the Cosmos Bag invented by Henry Cosmos. These soft cotton sandbags contained a small amount of radioactive ore. A bag was placed on top of an arthritic joint to bring relief.

The second product was radium water. People would buy a stoneware jug lined with radioactive ore and fill it with water overnight. The water became "radium water." Radium water was also available pre-bottled under the name of Radithor. Many doctors recommended it as a tonic, saying it had an invigorating effect. U.S. steel manufacturer Eben Beyers drank 1,400 bottles of Radithor before becoming fatally sick from radiation poisoning. He had to have his cancerous jaw and part of his mouth cut out before he died in 1932. The notice of his death in the *New York Times*, which mentioned Radithor, had a negative effect on the product's popularity.

Justice for the "Radium Girls"

Industrial uses of radium increased at the beginning of the 20th century. One U.S. company used a mixture that included radium to paint watch dials that would glow in the dark. During the 1920s court action was taken against the company after some of the women workers developed radiation poisoning.

Eventually the "Radium Girls," as the newspapers called them, received financial compensation. When news of the case was reported to Marie Curie in Paris, she could give little hope for their long-term health, saying, "There is absolutely no means of destroying the substance [radium] once it enters the human body." Curie herself died of radiation poisoning in 1934.

Radium was also used in the United Kingdom to paint numbers on clocks. These women are at work in the Ingersoll Watch and Clock Factory in London in 1932.

Medical radiation machines

After World War II, doctors started to use medical radiation machines to give doses of radiation to patients to destroy cancerous tumors. Doctors were aware by that time of the potential dangers of radiation. They were very careful that they made sure the right level of radiation was given, depending on the type of cancer cells being targeted.

Getting it wrong: Therac-25

By the time the Therac-25 radiotherapy machine was introduced in 1983, the Canadian company that made it had already experienced success with earlier models. This machine was built to deliver two different forms of radiation therapy as a cancer treatment: low-dose electron beams or high-dose mega X-ray therapy. However, in 1985 the first of at least six overexposure accidents caused by a computer software error took place. Over the next two years these incidents in the United States and Canada resulted in the deaths of at least four patients. Eventually the company was ordered to halt the use of these machines and to comply with government-ordered corrective action plans (CAP). Also, a number of lawsuits from the injured patients were settled out of court.

What was learned?

Once the machines were shut down, work began to find out how life-saving machines had been allowed to cause death. Particular attention was paid to the evidence given by the main users of the machines, hospital technicians and medical physicists (see box on page 31). The findings from the report into the Therac-25 accidents identified three areas of failure:

- Software errors: These were the actual cause of the extreme overexposure (100 times the normal dose) of the patients being treated.

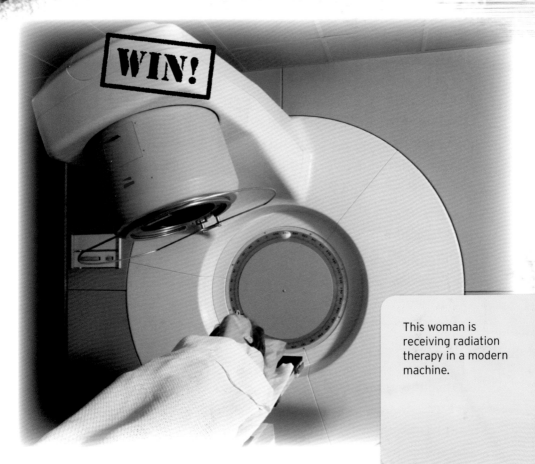

This woman is receiving radiation therapy in a modern machine.

- Company or institutional mistakes: Failure to accept that the machines were capable of overexposure, failure to recognize the need for more organized responses to reports of possible problems, and failure to communicate with users and regulatory authorities all contributed to the problem.

- Engineering mistakes: The reuse of some systems from previous Therac models combined with some untested new features were important engineering failures. Also, unlike the previous two models, the way the Therac-25 was built meant it relied totally on the correct operation of its software, with no protective hardware backup systems.

Medical physicists

Medical physicists or radiation physicists work for hospitals or health authorities. They use their knowledge of applied physics and technical skills in the medical use of radiotherapy, nuclear medicine, and **diagnostic** radiology.

Today, newspapers and television report every time a hospital is found to be the source of a dangerous infection, such as **MRSA** or **C-difficile**, or if the cleaning methods are found to be below standard. Around 150 years ago, not only were hospitals usually dark and filthy places, but most doctors also did not realize that it was bad hygiene that was killing many of their patients.

Blood equals experience

In the mid-19th century, doctors did not usually wear any special clothing that could be easily cleaned or replaced. They dressed in the normal clothes worn by people of their class. The only exceptions were the long aprons worn by surgeons, but these were to keep their street clothes from getting stained, not to protect their patients!

At this time, many surgeons refused to let their operating aprons be washed. After most operations the aprons would be splattered with blood and soaked in sweat. A heavily stained apron was prized because it showed that a surgeon was experienced and had performed many operations.

Surely dirt can't hurt

Even the most highly respected medical professionals, such as the well-known German surgeon Johann von Nussbaum, could not understand how up to 80 percent of their patients could die following technically perfect operations. Von Nussbaum described the terrible infections that his patients developed after surgery as "gnawing at every wound like an animal." At the time, doctors did not know that these often deadly infections could be lessened or prevented.

This team of surgeons from the early 20th century wore long aprons to keep their clothes free of blood stains.

Semmelweis tries to figure it out

In 1846 a young Hungarian doctor started work in Vienna, Austria, in a hospital with two public maternity clinics. His name was Ignaz Semmelweis. As an **obstetric** specialist, Semmelweis was well aware that childbirth was a dangerous time for both mother and child. One of the striking things about the two clinics in Vienna was that one had a much higher death rate than the other.

Ignaz Semmelweis was born in Buda (now Budapest), Hungary, in 1818. He died in Vienna in 1865.

Proving the dead caused death

As a doctor, Semmelweis felt humiliated that the **postpartum** death rate at his clinic, Clinic 1, was much higher than that in Clinic 2. Mothers who came for the free care were so frightened of its reputation that they preferred to give birth in the street outside, rather than risk entering Clinic 1. Semmelweis was even more upset by the fact that Clinic 1 was staffed by doctors and medical students, while the more successful Clinic 2 was run by midwives.

So Semmelweis started, in an organized and systematic way, to try to figure out why these additional deaths were happening. He collected statistics and considered many different factors. He found that even women giving birth in the street had a better survival rate than those in Clinic 1. What could be the factor that made Clinic 1 such a death trap? Then he realized the answer: it was the doctors themselves.

Within Clinic 1, doctors and medical students were performing **autopsies** and dissecting the bodies of women who had died of a widespread condition called puerperal fever (see box below). They would then examine or assist in the delivery of babies of living women, transferring the infection and other decaying matter from the dead bodies. Although Semmelweis did not really understand how the infection spread, he knew he had conclusively proved that it was happening.

Wash your hands!

When the doctors in Clinic 1 were told by Semmelweis to wash their hands in chloride of lime before examining living patients, the death rate there fell rapidly. Despite this, many doctors resented his interference and the personal hygiene regime. Although he eventually published his findings, Semmelweis was not taken seriously. His appointment at the clinic in Vienna was ended in 1849.

What is puerperal fever?

The deadly infection that Ignaz Semmelweis fought in Vienna is also known as childbirth fever. A woman who has just given birth, had an abortion, or had a miscarriage may get an infection in her uterus. If the infection spreads to her bloodstream it can cause blood poisoning, called septicemia. This condition, together with a dangerously high fever, was called puerperal fever in Semmelweis's time. Today, better hygiene and the availability of **antibiotics** mean that such infections are usually not fatal.

Hospital survival

During the Crimean War (1853–1856), the nurse Florence Nightingale made many observations about hospitals and the way they were run. She was head nurse in the hospital at Scutari, Turkey, where she noted that the number of soldiers dying of diseases and hygiene issues in the hospital was far higher than the number killed in battle. Her view was that good nutrition, cleanliness, proper sanitation and water supplies, organization, and efficiency were as important as medical treatments. With the changes she made, the Barracks Hospital in Scutari saw its death rate fall from 42 percent of those admitted to 2 percent by 1856.

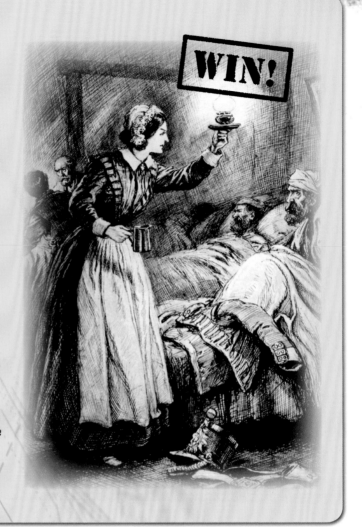

What was learned?

Thousands of women's lives would have been saved if medical workers had accepted Semmelweis's findings in the 1840s. Instead he spent the rest of his unhappy life fighting against hospital authorities and medical professionals. It was not until after his death that Semmelweis was finally vindicated, when the germ theories of first Louis Pasteur and then Robert Koch gained wider acceptance (see page 43). The medical world had continued dangerous practices by ignoring Semmelweis's scientifically collected evidence and logical conclusions.

By the early 20th century, hospitals began to pride themselves on their cleanliness. Nurses wore uniforms that were clean and changed regularly, and no surgeon would consider wearing bloody clothing in the operating room. Today, with increased worries about **bacteria** that are **resistant** to cleaning methods, doctors, patients, and visitors are being required to follow tight new hygiene rules. These include the use of special hand gels and doctors being forbidden to wear long ties or other loose garments that could carry infection from one patient to another.

Doctors and other medical personnel must put hygiene at the top of their priorities if they want their patients to recover.

WIN!

Miasma: Clouds of Disease

For thousands of years, human beings have tried to make sense of the world they live in. They have observed phenomena around them and tried to understand how and why things happened. Some things were easy to figure out. For example, when there was a drought, plants did not grow and even died. Therefore, plants needed water to grow. Other things were more difficult, such as why some people grew sick and died when they were young and others lived to old age. Why did some diseases strike down just one person and others kill hundreds in a short period of time? Over the years, theories accepted as truth were used to explain how things worked and why things happened. One theory that was treated as a proven fact was the miasma theory of the spread of disease.

It's all in the air

As far back as the time of the ancient Greeks, miasma, which is the Greek word for "pollution," was used to explain the spread of disease. It was believed that poisonous "bad air" caused diseases such as cholera, typhoid, and plague. The bad air was thought to contain fine particles, known as miasmata. They thought it was the inhaling of miasmata that caused a person to get sick.

Bad smell equals sickness

This view of how diseases were spread continued to be an accepted belief for over 2,000 years. In the **Middle Ages** more emphasis was put on the foul odor thought to accompany a miasma. It was believed that noxious gases mixed with fumes from decayed matter to create the stink of a miasma. Doctors told people that they would be protected by smelling sweet fragrances, and people also used candles and torches to clear the air.

A miasma of Black Death

During the 14th century, there was an outbreak throughout Europe of a disease called the plague, also known as the Black Death. The disease was so terrible that it must have been comforting to try anything that might help. During the outbreak, doctors wore strange outfits when visiting their patients. They were covered from head to foot so that the "bad air" could not touch them, and they breathed through a beak-like opening in a special hood. The beak was kept full of sweet-smelling herbs or sponges soaked in vinegar. The stronger the smell, the better.

Doctors believed this strange outfit would protect them from catching the plague.

Cracks in the miasma theory

For nearly 2,000 years the miasma theory helped doctors explain how they thought diseases spread. As scientific knowledge advanced, and as the technology of science improved, other options were revealed. From the 17th century onward, improvements in lenses made it possible for microscopes to see smaller and smaller things, including very small living things.

The four humors

For many years, the inner workings of the human body were explained through the theory of the "four humors." The four humors were phlegm, blood, black bile, and yellow bile. Good health depended on having the right amounts of each humor in your body. If the balance of the humors were disturbed, this could cause a weakness or illness. If a doctor thought you were suffering from a condition that related to having too much blood, for example, then he would bleed you by opening up a vein and filling a bowl. People believed that this would restore the balance.

This 16th-century picture shows the four humors in the form of four men: black bile (top left), blood (top right), yellow bile (bottom left), and phlegm (bottom right). In the middle is the head of Christ.

Some doctors began to consider whether these living organisms could play a part in infection and disease. However, a 2,000-year-old theory was not just going to lie down and die. Right up to the mid-19th century, the miasma theory had very strong supporters who would not consider other causes for diseases. One such group of miasma theory supporters were the politicians and doctors in Britain who campaigned for public health.

No stink, no disease?

These medical and political campaigners, including Sir Edwin Chadwick and Sir John Simon, were passionate about the need to improve the living conditions of the urban poor. Improved water networks and sewage systems would rid areas of their foul stench. As firm believers in the miasma theory, they thought that health would improve as the foul smell cleared. In Chadwick's report of 1842 on the spread of disease among London's slum dwellers, he said "**Epidemic** disease amongst the labouring classes is caused by atmospheric impurities…"

This picture, dating from the mid-19th century, shows the overcrowded and dirty living conditions of the poor.

John Snow and the Soho pump handle

What is epidemiology?

Epidemiology is the systematic study of the causes, frequency, and distribution of diseases in a population. Dr. John Snow's pioneering work in tracing the source of a disease by mapping its spread has led to him being referred to as one of the first epidemiologists.

In 1854 there was an outbreak of the deadly disease cholera in London. This disease caused such severe diarrhea that it usually led to death. The accepted view was that cholera was an airborne disease. However, London doctor John Snow did not believe in miasma as a cause of disease. In 1849 he had written an article presenting his theory that cholera was a disease that entered the body through the mouth. The article did not generate much interest. When the cholera outbreak occurred, Snow plotted every case of the disease on a map and showed where he thought the disease originated—a public water pump in London's Soho neighborhood. When the pump handle was removed, making the pump unusable, the number of cases went down. The cholera was in the water, not in the air.

This 1854 map of the Soho area of London shows where the deaths from cholera occurred. Most of them were around the water pump on Broad Street.

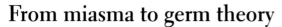

From miasma to germ theory

Most doctors in the 19th century accepted that there were microbes known as germs, but they thought these microbes were the result of disease, not the cause of it. Experiments done by Louis Pasteur between 1857 and 1867 proved the connection between germs and disease. However, even after Pasteur performed his experiments at public demonstrations, some doctors refused to accept the germ theory of disease.

Robert Koch was a German doctor and researcher who took germ theory a step further by gradually identifying which microbes caused which diseases. He identified the microbe that caused anthrax in 1876, tuberculosis in 1882, and cholera in 1883.

What was learned?

Koch's exceptional work identifying the actual microbes that cause a disease finally led to the end of the miasma theory. This showed the importance of experimental proofs and understanding the epidemiology (see box on page 42) of the spread of diseases. It also opened the door for the science of disease prevention, and for the development of real, effective cures.

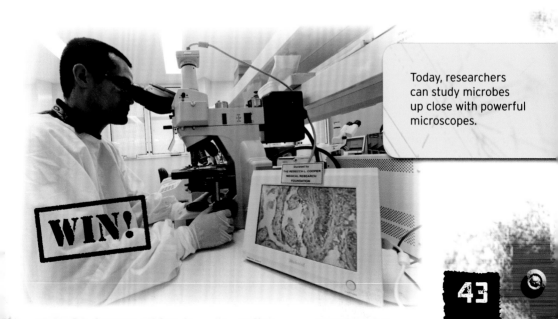

Today, researchers can study microbes up close with powerful microscopes.

WIN!

Tobacco: From Cure-All to Kill-All

When men working for the 16th-century writer and adventurer Sir Walter Raleigh returned to England after the long journey to the **New World**, they brought dried tobacco plants back with them. With Raleigh and other men at court smoking the tobacco, its popularity soon spread, first throughout the highest levels of society, then to all classes. The habit of tobacco use was already thousands of years old by the time it came to Europe. It was first cultivated by native peoples in Central America and then spread north and south. By the start of the first millennium CE, the growing and use of tobacco had covered the Americas. It was smoked, sniffed, and chewed.

Pipe, not plant

The name *tobacco* comes from a Native American word for the central tube of a calumet, which is a ceremonial pipe. When Europeans first interacted with native peoples, they were often offered an opportunity to smoke a calumet. When the Europeans were given the pipe, they thought the word being spoken—*tobacco*—referred to the substance in the pipe, rather than part of the pipe itself. Their mistake gave the tobacco plant its common name.

This painting, dating from the 18th century, shows a fashionable man smoking tobacco in a pipe.

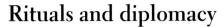

Rituals and diplomacy

Among the peoples of the Americas, tobacco was used for specific purposes, mainly political and religious. It was thought to be powerful, **hallucinogenic**, and even magical. This meant that its use was limited and controlled by those in power. For this reason, in these societies tobacco never achieved widespread usage.

When you think about it now, it is hard to understand how such a strange activity ever caught on. The first of the Spanish explorers in the New World described the smoking of dried tobacco in a type of cigar form. It looked to them like a musket (a kind of gun) that was then set on fire at one end, with the user "drinking" in the smoke. In 1492 a member of Christopher Columbus's crew, Rodrigo de Jerez, became the first European to be a tobacco smoker.

A cure for hiccups?

From the 16th century, the use of tobacco in pipes, cigars, and eventually cigarettes became widespread. During the next 300 years, tobacco was generally approved by the medical authorities. Some individual doctors forcefully put forward their reservations, but others recommended tobacco as a cure for all ills. These included hiccups, jaundice, syphilis, obesity, and mental retardation. In addition to doctors' recommendations that patients smoke it, tobacco was also made into other medical products, such as pills, oils, plasters, balms or creams, and **poultices**.

Healthy lungs?

During the plague in the 1660s, British doctors recommended smoking tobacco to ward off the miasma of plague in the air. By the 19th century, smoking tobacco was seen as a way to clear the lungs. Some doctors even believed that smoking tobacco in a pipe could cure asthma. They thought the smoke in the lungs would allow asthmatics to breathe more freely. The truth is that tobacco smoke damages the lining of the lungs' bronchial tubes and makes damaged airways heal more slowly. All of these ideas for the use of tobacco were made without any reliable evidence, proper trials, or scientific analysis of results.

Unstoppable

It is not surprising that tobacco's popularity continued to grow in the 19th and 20th centuries:

- It was believed to treat or cure many different ills, including stress and bad nerves.
- It contained chemical substances that were very addictive, making it hard for people to stop using it once they started.
- It was becoming more and more important to the economies of many countries.

After the development of a mechanical cigarette roller, cigarettes became more affordable, and the number of smokers around the world shot up. By the 1930s cigarette smoking had become the most popular form of tobacco usage. For example, in 1900, 2.5 billion cigarettes a year were sold in the United States.

Early medical voices against tobacco

Some doctors were concerned from the very beginning that tobacco could be dangerous to health. A Scottish doctor, Eleazar Duncon, was convinced that tobacco was particularly addictive and harmful to the young. He suggested that it should be called "Youth-bane," meaning it was likely to cause misery or harm to youth. By 1798 U.S. Dr. Benjamin Rush, one of the signers of the Declaration of Independence, was convinced that use of tobacco should be severely limited. Neither of these men, however, made much of an impact on the attitudes of their profession.

By 1940 the annual figure for cigarettes sold was 182 billion. Around 371 billion cigarettes were sold in the United States in 2006.

No evidence?

During World War II, the cigarette was still king. Doctors and military authorities recommended smoking for soothing battle-weary nerves and to keep tropical insects at bay. However, some medical professionals were starting to question the increasing health problems that seemed linked to tobacco use. As early as 1912, U.S. doctor Isaac Adler suggested that tobacco use directly caused lung cancer. By 1929 German doctor Fritz Lickint had collected statistics that suggested the same thing. It was not until the 1944 report of the American Society for the Control of Cancer (later the American Cancer Society) on the negative effects of smoking that it really started to become an area for medical research. However, even the report admitted "no definite evidence exists" to link smoking with cancer. Doctors were still careful not to make any claims against smoking that they could not prove.

During the first half of the 20th century, it was perfectly normal for most adults, including doctors, to smoke.

Statistics from doctors

In the 1950s the medical tide turned against smoking, but the damage was already done. A highly addictive substance considered by some to be of grave danger to health was the **recreational drug** of millions of people. The popularity of the cigarette seemed unstoppable. In 1956 the first results of a questionnaire called the British Doctors Study were published. It used health information provided by British doctors to decide if smoking affected health or life expectancy. The results overwhelmingly tied smoking to lung cancer and heart disease. It also seemed to show that being a smoker made an individual die at least 10 years earlier than a nonsmoker, even if the smoker developed no obvious disease.

In 1964 the U.S. Surgeon General (the chief medical officer of the United States), Luther Terry, published *Smoking and Health: Report of the Advisory Committee to the Surgeon General*. This exhaustive study reported that in any one year a smoker was 70 percent more likely to die than a nonsmoker. Terry described the effect of his commission's report as "like a bombshell." The information was now public knowledge, and the debate about smoking increased.

Trying to fight back

In the mid-1950s tobacco companies decided that if doctors were going to turn against tobacco, the companies needed to fight back. They set up the Council for Tobacco Research with their own doctors and statisticians. It published statistics that seemed to show that tobacco was not causing illnesses and death. However, governments and medical bodies were not going to back down.

Smoking-related deaths

Worldwide deaths in developed countries, 1930s to 1990s:

1930–59	11 million
1960–69	9 million
1970–79	13 million
1980–89	17 million
1990–99	21 million

Legal action was taken against tobacco product manufacturers, and health warnings and messages became stronger and more straightforward. For example, the first warnings printed on cigarette packages said, "Smoking may damage your health." By the 1980s some countries printed tough phrases, such as "Smokers die young." Tobacco advertising was banned for sports and on television in most places.

The British scientist Richard Doll (pictured) pioneered research into the links between smoking and lung cancer in 1950.

No more doubt

After over 400 years of supporting tobacco use or appearing to be unconcerned about its effects, from the mid-1960s most doctors went all out against smoking. Governments followed suit. During the last 40 years, attempts have been made using the law, taxation, and persuasion to get people in the developed world to stop smoking. It is no longer considered as socially acceptable or glamorous as it was in the 1940s and 1950s. Many places do not allow smoking in public places, including on public transportation or in restaurants. Unfortunately the number of people in the world threatening their health with tobacco is still increasing, particularly as the habit is still growing in the developing world. Around 40 percent of all current cigarette smokers in the world live in China.

Timeline

2000–1500 BCE	Earliest ancient Egyptian medical writings
460–375 BCE	Life of Greek physician Hippocrates, the "father of medicine"
384–322 BCE	Life of Greek thinker Aristotle. He introduces the theory of the four humors.
c. 129–200 CE	Life of Greek doctor Galen. His work influences doctors until the **Middle Ages**.
980–1037	Life of Avicenna (Ibn Fina), most famous of the early Islamic doctors. His writings influence Western doctors for hundreds of years to come.
1347–1351	Black Death (plague) kills an estimated 25 million people in Europe
1492	Tobacco first introduced to Europeans
1664–1666	Great Plague in London kills an estimated 100,000 people
1728	Death of Dr. Hugh Chamberlen means that the design of the Chamberlen forceps becomes public
1796	English doctor Edward Jenner introduces his **vaccination** against smallpox
1800–1890	Life of Edwin Chadwick, the British politician who campaigned for public health and sanitation
1818–1865	Life of Ignaz Semmelweiss, the Hungarian **obstetrician** who discovered that doctors were spreading disease
1843–1910	Life of German medical researcher Robert Koch, who developed and proved the germ theory of disease
1845	U.S. dentist Horace Wells first uses anesthetic to relieve pain

1854	Dr. John Snow figures out that water is responsible for the spread of cholera
1854–1915	Life of German medical researcher Paul Ehrlich, who developed chemotherapy
1855	Florence Nightingale starts the reform of British nursing and military conditions
1870s	Joseph Lister's antiseptic spray is widely used in operations from this time
1885	Louis Pasteur develops immunization against rabies in humans
1895	Wilhelm Roentgen makes the first X-ray image
1928	British medical researcher Alexander Fleming discovers penicillin. By 1942 it has been developed into a useful **antibiotic** by Howard Florey and Ernst Chain.
1944	American Society for the Control of Cancer's report on the effects of smoking is published
1954	German drug company develops thalidomide
1956	British Doctors Study questionnaire results on smoking is published
1961	Thalidomide is withdrawn from use
1964	*Smoking and Health: Report of the Advisory Committee to the Surgeon General* is published
1967	South African doctor Christiaan Barnard performs the first successful heart transplant
1978	First test-tube baby is born
1983	**HIV** identified as the virus that can lead to **AIDS**
1985	First overexposure accident by the Therac-25 radiotherapy machine
2003	Mapping of the human genome is completed

Glossary

addictive causing a physical dependence

anemia not having enough iron in the blood

antibiotic substance used to fight bacterial infections

antipsychotic able to control psychosis, a mental condition in which a person loses touch with reality

autopsy examination of a body after death

bacteria microscopic organisms. Some bacteria can cause diseases.

C-difficile *Clostridium difficile*, a hard-to-treat bacterial infection that causes diarrhea

cognitive behavioral therapy (CBT) talking therapy used to understand and change how a person thinks and behaves

colonial America period between 1492 and 1763 when settlers from Europe came to live in America

diagnostic something used to figure out, or diagnose, what a disease is or what caused it

epidemic disease that rapidly becomes widespread

ethics moral principles or special rules of conduct

gene part of a person's biological makeup that determines inherited characteristics

hallucinogenic mind-altering; causing one to have illusions

HIV/AIDS (Human Immunodeficiency Virus/Acquired Immune Deficiency Syndrome) HIV is a virus that damages the human immune system. AIDS is a condition that is caused by HIV, and which leaves the body open to attack by infectious diseases.

hypothesis theory or unproven idea

immune system system that helps the body to avoid and fight off infections and diseases

incontinence loss of the ability to control urination and defecation

Industrial Revolution when Great Britain, the United States, and other countries were transformed from agricultural into industrial nations in the 18th and 19th centuries

inoculation inducing a mild form of a disease to produce immunity

Middle Ages period of European history from the fall of the western Roman Empire in 500 CE to the 16th century

misdiagnose figure out the wrong disease from the symptoms

morning sickness nausea with vomiting that often occurs during the first three months of pregnancy

MRSA Methicillin-resistant *Staphylococcus aureus*, a hard-to-treat bacterial infection causing, among other symptoms, boils and fever

New World North and South American continents, first explored by Europeans in the late 15th century

oath form of words spoken to confirm belief in something

obstetrics specialized area of medicine dealing with childbirth and the care of women and children before and after childbirth

patent exclusive right of an inventor to make and sell an invention

pharmaceutical to do with drugs

placenta organ in the uterus that provides a fetus with nutrition during pregnancy

postpartum after a birth

poultice soft, moist material, containing herbs, tobacco, or bran, strapped onto an affected area of the body to aid its recovery

professional jealousy possessiveness related to professional expertise

recreational drug substance used non-medically for enjoyment that alters normal body and brain responses

resistant able to oppose or hinder; not affected by

sanatorium hospital or health center for people suffering from chronic illness

schizophrenia mental disorder, often involving hallucinations

vaccination giving a vaccine as a protection against catching disease

vivisection operating on a living animal for the purposes of experimentation or research

Find Out More

Books

Bingham, Jane. *Smoking* (*What's the Deal* series). Chicago: Heinemann Library, 2006.

Morgan, Sally. *Germ Killers: Fighting Disease* (*Science at the Edge* series). Chicago: Heinemann Library, 2009.

Reid, Struan. *Florence Nightingale* (*Lives and Times* series). Chicago: Heinemann Library, 2005.

Senker, Cath. *The Black Death: 1347–1350* (*When Disaster Struck* series). Chicago: Raintree, 2007.

Websites

www.sc.edu/library/spcoll/nathist/jenner.html
Check out this website for more information about Edward Jenner and the development of vaccination.

www.cdc.gov/tb/
Learn more about tuberculosis at this Centers for Disease Contol and Prevention (CDC) website.

www.who.int/topics/tobacco/en/
Find out more facts about tobacco use at this World Health Organization (WHO) website.

Further research

The failures described in this book, the lessons that were learned, and the successes that sometimes followed raise issues that you can explore further. Here are some ideas for areas to find out more about:

- the history of medicine
- more about the lives of people involved in the events covered
- infectious diseases and developments in the field of epidemiology
- vaccination and immunization
- the battle to find a way to cure or prevent HIV/AIDS
- mental health issues and how we view mental illness
- the differences in medical care available in richer and poorer areas of the world
- the growing problem of gene "patenting" by drug companies and scientific researchers
- the ways in which governments, doctors, and others are trying to get people to stop smoking, or to never start at all

Index